Dedication

This book is dedicated to my three beautiful ladybugs, JaMiya, Jayla, & Cortai, who have given me more strength during my darkest hours than they know. I hope each of you understands that you are worthy, and fearfully and wonderfully made. As you continue to put God first, know that I will always be there to cheer you on. Just know that no matter what life throws, things will always work out for your good. Mommy loves you! To God be the Glory!

Table of Contents

Chapter 1: At Birth 1

Chapter 2: The Drug Dealer...................................11

Chapter 3: High School Heartbreak 17

Chapter 4: Age Ain't Nothing But A Number.............23

Chapter 5: The Storm...29

Chapter 6: I Didn't Know My Own Strength 43

Chapter 7: A Piece of the Puzzle...............................51

Chapter 8: A Few Good Men 57

Chapter 9: My Bestie 65

Chapter 10: Not Again 71

Chapter 11: The One...81

CHAPTER 1

At Birth

(Jeremiah 1:5 "Before I formed you in the womb I knew you, before you were born I set you apart; I appointed you as a prophet to the nations.")

Mom probably had no idea about the joy and pain she was bringing into the world. Was her unknown pain passed onto me while in her womb, just as the nutrients I received thru the umbilical cord? The birth of a child is always supposed to be a joyous occasion for a family. Tradition says, 'love, marriage, and then a baby carriage'. Well, that theory doesn't apply to every situation.

After hours of pain, a beautiful baby girl was birthed into the world. The family was proud…well, almost everyone. My uncle, Maurice, was upset because his title had been taken. He was no longer the baby in the house. You see, we lived with my maternal grandparents and I was getting all of the attention. There were always multiple stories told around the family dinner that were sure to make you laugh. Some of the stories were true and others were often made up. One of the stories told was that my Uncle Maurice was so upset that there was a new baby on board that he tried to flush me down the toilet. Was he really going to flush me down the toilet? Naw, he loves me too much to do that! My parents didn't stick together too long after my birth. Was that my fault? Well, hold tight baby girl, because that answer will be revealed later in life.

Mom and dad went into two different directions, which led dad to someone else. I was never sure if his first wife was fond of me because I didn't have memories of being in their home when I was little. I was not sure if that was my mother's decision, my father's decision, or the typical woman dislike syndrome. The typical woman dislike syndrome means 'I don't like your ex-girlfriend and don't like your child either'.

At a young age, I questioned why my dad left and started a new family, but I'm glad he did, because it gave me a sister. I was too young to fully understand the process and never saw dad enough to know the difference. I guarantee you mom knew the difference and likely still feels it today. Was this the beginning of a generational curse? Well, mom's journey took her away from me for a while because she had to figure out a way to provide a better future for us. My mom joined the military and served our country, and my grandparents were left with the responsibility to take care of me.

I was in elementary school and could not understand the "adult stuff". I had my toys and my grandparents, and that was all I needed. Thank God for blessing me with good grandparents. I could not go and live with my dad because he had his new life with his wife. Needless to say, my mother was not having that. There was too much tension between my mom and dad in the beginning. I stayed with my paternal grandparents until mom returned from the military. I was in a loving two-parent environment and was getting spoiled, so life was great. My aunts lived there also, so, I was extra spoiled because of their love, too. I was the first grandbaby on my dad's side, so I was never told "no" often. My paternal grandfather would take me to school and take my paternal grandmother to work. Let's just say the car rides were interesting to say the least. I recall being in the car with them and my grandfather was listening to the radio. He had his cigarette, large cup of water, and his hat on. Yes, my grandfather was the best to me. He was in the car chilling while listening to the radio. Here comes his queen getting into the car. As she was entering, I was praying for the Lord to let there be peace in this car ride. You see my grandmother always had a "honey-do" list for my grandfather while she was at work. He worked nights and she worked in the daytime. I don't even recall if he received his instructions this particular morning. As I reflect back, I think he turned the radio on as a way of tuning my grandmother out. She gets in the car and the first thing she does is turn the station to what she wanted to hear. He turned it back and she turned it again. He said, "Woman, you always doing something". She looked at him as if she was innocent and replied "what?" Yes, she turned the station again and then my grandfather uttered his famous line.

"Aw shit, Marlene".

She replied, "Not in front of the baby, Ralph".

This car ride still makes me laugh today. You see, it showed me that love can conquer all and marriages do last until death do them apart. As much as they got on each other's nerves, I knew they loved one another.

I always saw my aunts, uncles, cousins, and family friends because my grandmother was always frying chicken or something. I just don't recall seeing my dad. No, he was not on drugs or in jail; he just chose not to be there often enough for me. I was his child, so what happened to seeing me every day? I mean he came around briefly at times to visit my grandparents and aunts, but I don't recall my dad being there for me.

Well, mom returned from being all she could be, and back home I went. My paternal grandparents still got me on weekends and for summer vacations. Yet still, I was not with my dad. He showed up for special occasions like my birthday and graduations, but never for the extra special moments. Those extra special moments like showing me how to tie my shoe, how to ride a bike, brush my teeth, or playing games. Thank goodness mom took plenty of pictures because I would not have known my dad was at my birthday parties. I guess that's because I was too young to remember. Cellphones were not even invented yet. Is the memory so vague because the impact was so little, or not enough film to capture each moment?

Great job mom, because I finally made it to middle school. At this point, mom was working two jobs because it wasn't just me anymore. There is something about a black mother who will risk it all for her child to have the best. It surely does take a village to raise a child and some prayers from grandma. (Thank God for my maternal family). My maternal grandmother would come home from working nights at the hospital and straight to the kitchen to fix us breakfast. She drank her cup of coffee while calling on the name of Jesus at least twenty times. Who was this Jesus? What was Jesus going to do? The strength of a woman was always visual for me because I saw my grandmother take care of her husband, nine children, and grandchildren. This marriage was different because my maternal grandfather was there, but not there as he should have been. Regardless of the cards dealt, my maternal grandmother made sure we stayed together (I remember my grandmother in a happy way). My family helped out a lot with taking us to school or babysitting; however, there came a time when mom began to rely on me. It's called 'you're the oldest child' syndrome. There is no medication to get rid of this condition. I began to do things for my siblings and the family still came around to support.

Still, I don't recall seeing dad often. He came by his parents' house and would stick around for a while, but no quality time was put in with me. I still went to visit with my grandparents. It was traditional for my paternal grandmother to get all of her grandchildren together for an annual photoshoot. We had pretty dresses, bows in our hair, and our edges were laid. It was important to my grandmother that my sister and I knew each other. Same dad but different mothers made no difference to me because it was simple… we were family. I often wonder how things would be if my paternal grandparents didn't intervene.

Now, things became interesting because high school, here I come! My family was still involved and helped my mom and siblings out; however, the responsibilities as the oldest child increased. I helped with homework, cooked sometimes, and did my sisters' hair to say the least. I managed to still excel in school and made achievements, but dad was still limited. So, I decided to get in trouble and test the one person who sacrificed the most. The one who worked three jobs, raised four children at the time, and still managed to provide. Yes, my mother. I became the typical teenager, who thought she knew it all. My mother asked me to do something and I began to talk back. She popped me with that 18" ruler and I hit her back. That was not a bright idea because when she swung back that's when I realized who Jesus was. She called my dad and told him to come get *his* child and let me move in with him. I'm thinking to myself, *Has she lost her mind? Because I don't want to live with my dad and his second wife.* Needless to say, I didn't leave, but I had to listen to this long, boring speech from my dad. I hated those long speeches. This speech included a car ride down to Baltimore Street. Baltimore Street is a block where you will see prostitutes, bars, and strip joints. Did I mention the police department headquarters is in the next block over?

Part of being a teenager is being hormonal. I was never one to have a lot of boyfriends, nor was I fast in the pants. I just liked the attention and the compliments I received. You see, I was never told I was beautiful or that I had greatness within me. I never met my designated first love, which was supposed to be my dad. So, I participated in activities in high school to try to keep me sane. Let's see- four years in high school, countless games to cheer, and parades to march in….but where was dad? The first heartbreaking moment of my life occurred on a special day. My dad's co-worker walked onto the football field and said, "Hey, I work with your dad." I stood there with a crazy look on my face because I didn't know who this tall, black man was. I never met him a day in my life. The man said, "He told me you would likely be here." In my mind, I said *well, where is he?* I actually was getting a little excited because I was thinking he made it to the event. My dad finally made it to see one of my games before I finished high school. Well, that was not the case. I was so disappointed and hurt on the inside. I had to hold my feelings inside and smile on the outside. I could do that because that's what cheerleaders do. This is where I learned to hold your feelings to yourself because the one you want it to matter to likely won't even care. Now, refocus girlie, because you have to cheer your team on and check out that fine player on the opposing team at the same time!

Well, Dad finally showed up at my graduation. At this point in life, the tension seemed to die down. I really didn't understand as a child what the tension was between my mom and dad. As a child, I only knew that my parents were not married. I never heard my mother say anything bad about my dad. My graduation was the one moment that I did not expect to let go of the pain from my childhood or so I thought. Dad walked to my mom and told her "Thank you. You have done a wonderful job raising our daughter." I had to respect my dad for recognizing the struggle my mom endured. More importantly, my mom looked as if she just received a crown. She smiled with a sigh of relief. I guess she was thinking, 'One down, three to go'. So congratulations mom, you did it! I just had to figure out what's next because I was off to a different world.

CHAPTER 2

The Drug Dealer

(Psalm 23:4 "Even though I walk through the darkest valley, I will fear no evil, for you are with me; your rod and your staff, they comfort me" NIV)

The drug and crime epidemics have overshadowed the greatness of Baltimore so much so that it could be said that people have become numb to it. There are so many challenges that families face and finances is one. The concept of a microwaveable response to getting quick money unfortunately calls many young boys and girls to the street corner. It's the quick cash, fancy clothes, and flashy things that can draw a young girl into the arms of a drug dealer.

"Hey shorty, what's your name?" You see, with not having the proper foundation instilled in me at a young aged, I automatically responded. I mean, why not? Monty was flashy. He wasn't the best looking one on the block, but he gave me attention. He made me feel as if I was the most beautiful girl in the village. Far too often young females get caught up in the images they see on television. It was cool because he had the image of a "ruff-neck". A ruff neck is a guy with street swag. I responded with my name and it went on from there. We talked and the conversation seemed to always lead to some type of sexual conversation. What happened to the conversation regarding my dreams, my flaws, or my fears? I guess that type of conversation was out the door. Anyway, I just played along as if I knew what Monty was talking about. I had no clue. I was a virgin and couldn't even tell you what a condom was or how to use it at the time, if you paid me. Dad was never consistently around and mom was always working, so that left me in the hands of a man when I was just a girl. I had just finished the 8th grade and Monty was ten years older than me. I think the most he ever bought me was a chicken box. Yes, I had salt, pepper, and ketchup on everything. Wait, that fool didn't even get me a half and half…LOL! It's a Baltimore thing.

A chicken box from Edmondson Village was like eating at a famous upscale seafood restaurant. Monty would come over and would leave, but I still would not have sex with him. Yes, we kissed and hugged but that was it because I was too scared to go further. I will never forget the day gun shots rang out on the corner. I was just about to go to the corner store to get some sunflower seeds and sit on the porch to talk with my friends. I never knew until that day why my mother always told us to stay off the front. Shots were being fired and I was scared because everything was happening so fast. My three friends, including Monty's brother, ran into my house with me. Monty's brother left back out to check on Monty. After all the madness, it was determined that a close friend of theirs was killed. Even that crazy experience didn't keep me away from him. Bullets have no name on them and that could have been me had I gone to the corner store. I mean ladies, I had a man and that's all that should have mattered, right?

A few months later, Monty and I were walking from the corner store. The block was not even heavy with drug activity, yet it didn't stop the police from coming to do their rounds. On this calm day, a particular police officer who was familiar with Monty had stopped him. I was there and attempted to keep walking, but the officer stopped me too. I could have pissed on myself. Not because of the police officer, but because I knew my mother was going to kill me. I'm praying and holding my pee at the same time because I did not know if this fool had drugs on him. Thank goodness he didn't, and I didn't get searched because an important call came across the officer's radio. Guess what? I still stuck around because I was just content with having the comfort of a man. What could I possibly know about a man? Remember, I was only a child myself.

It finally got to a point where my mother met him, but she never knew his age. When she met him, he needed a place to stay. So I asked my mother and she said yes. I was so pumped because here I am in the tenth grade with my so-called boyfriend staying with me. There were a lot of rules in place for this to happen. We were not allowed to stay in the same room. It did not stop us from being sneaky. My mother always opens her heart up to help people. The day came when Monty was supposed to go get a chicken box, but apparently he grabbed the chicken box and lost his brain. He met this girl at the store and they exchanged numbers. This fool gave her my house number. The phone rings and a female asked to speak to Monty. Of course, I wanted to know who she was. She explained everything. I was not mad with her at all, but I kindly told Monty he had to leave. He called to try to apologize, but his best friend called me a bitch in the background. Monty did not even defend me. I knew then that I did not want to be with a man who could not stand up for me. After a period of reflection, I learned that a man whose conversation is always about sex is not the man for you. In a true relationship, your conversational topics should vary. A conversation always based on sex clearly indicates the other parties intention is just on that one thing. When you get to a point where you love yourself, things become clear. You learn what you will settle for and what you won't. Yes, girl you are powerful and valuable, and don't let no one tell you different. I also learned that God's hand of protection is always upon you. When you actually take a moment to look back over your life-especially your childhood to teenage years- you can be grateful for the many times God kept you. As I reflect, I am grateful for how he kept me from the seen and unseen dangers. Even when I was at the wrong place, at the wrong time, and with the wrong people, God still kept me. I guess even when I didn't know, someone else knew enough to keep me covered in prayer. Prayer is so powerful, and it works!

CHAPTER 3

High School Heartbreak

(John 15:13 "Greater love has no one than this, that someone lay down his life for his friends" ESV)

It was the fall of 1996, my senior year in high school. This was supposed to be one of the best years of my life. I had a crush on a young man, John, who attended my rival high school. John was fine in high school and unbeknownst to me, he was loved by the ladies. I struggled with my self-esteem and for some reason, I was confident whenever he was around. We mainly hung out on the weekends and when school was closed. Just about everyone at my school knew we were dating. At least, that's what I thought. In the spring of 1997, he accompanied another girl to her school dance. I was unaware at the time what was going on. A classmate informed me of the incident and I was more shocked than hurt. I didn't believe it in the beginning. I called John and he gave me his version, or should I say excuses. I forgave him immediately because he was my boyfriend and I trusted him. I should have just walked away then to avoid any further heartbreak moments down the road. I also accepted his excuse because it was familiar to me. What was so familiar about John's excuses? Well, I always felt like I received excuses from my dad. My dad would tell me he was busy working; however, as a teenager his rationale was becoming too repetitive. I always wondered if my dad was really swamped with work or was it something else that was preventing him from being more involved in my life. I would often wonder whether or not he could just sacrifice a day off for me, if he really worked all those hours, or why his wife and new family got time with him that I didn't.

My dad and I never established a strong foundation in the beginning. The foundation of opening the car door for me or giving me flowers simply just because. If only my dad would have been more involved in my life to explain things and contribute to enhancing my self-esteem, I could have spotted a joker a mile away and avoided guys like John. My first heartbreak really came from my dad, and all these years I thought John broke my heart first.

One of my special moments in high school was my senior prom. I met my dad at my paternal grandparents' house so they could see me and take a few quick pictures. I was so excited because my birthday, prom, and graduation were all within a two week timeframe. Life was good because I had my man to celebrate with- at least that's what I thought. A classmate came to me and told me that John went to the prom with the same girl from before. In my book, that's cheating. We got into a big argument and he cancelled attending my prom with me. I was so devastated. My heart was crushed. I laid my head in my mother's lap and cried. I did not want to come out of my room. I was so embarrassed because I did not think I was going to have a date to my senior prom. Everything for the prom was paid for. I was literally at the point of not even going. My mother's friend called John's dad to inform him what his son did. His dad personally apologized. While I appreciated the apology, it did not take my pain away. My god-brother, Tavon, came through for me. He hung in there with the vest being too tight for him and all. He did that just for me and I was grateful, but I still felt a sense of emptiness. The truth is, the glass was never full. It had been empty since birth, but I did not realize that at the time. My 18th birthday, senior prom, and graduation were bittersweet because the one person I wanted there completely disappeared. I made it thru the summer with a broken heart and managed to see John later on. In the past, I always told myself that I would slap him when I saw him. I just looked at him while calling him everything I could think of in my mind. Let's just say they were not nice thoughts. I spoke to his brother as he was standing next to him. John spoke and I just ignored him. I was still carrying anger because of what he did.

In the fall of 1997, we were embracing college. I started off at a local community college and John went to a local university. I received a call from him one day and we talked on the phone for hours. During the conversation, he said let's finish this conversation face to face. Of course, I went to talk to him. We sat in my car for hours. Before I realized it, it was 5:00 a.m. and I had to be to work at 6 a.m. I could not believe I sat there all that time. I guess you are wondering what we could have possibly talked about all that time. Well, I listened to him apologize and trying to justify his wrong. I was so caught up in the moment that I forgot about what's important...ME. I had worked the day before at my full time job and then went to school. When I came home, I never had a chance to rest. I showered up and lay in the bed talking to John on the phone before meeting at the university. I left the university at 5:00 a.m. I was so tired and could barely stay awake, and I fell asleep behind the wheel of my green BMW on Howard and North Avenue. It was cold outside this particular night and I had the heat blasting in the car. Yes, I was warm and getting comfortable.

Perhaps too comfortable, but I could not afford to be late for work was all I was thinking. The radio was off in the car and before I knew it I fell asleep behind the wheel. Boom! Screech! What was that? I had awakened in shock because of the impact. I just rear ended a car at a red light. I was just minutes away from work. Why couldn't I just have stayed awake long enough to make it to the office? Why did I even agree to meet with John? The police came to the scene and my co-worker picked me up to take me to the hospital. The other driver did not sustain any injuries and was very polite to me. I suffered a concussion and minor contusions. Look at God still protecting me even in my mess! I was calling on Jesus yet again because I did not want to face my mother. I called John to let him know what happened to see if he would come to my house after his classes. He told me he was not available and hung the phone up. I never heard back from him. I risked my life and he refused to come see me or hold me to let me feel secure. I put my life on the line because I didn't recognize my worth at the time.

I ran into John ten years later downtown. He had a few drinks and felt the need to confess his sins to me. He claimed that I was too mature for him at the time and he was not ready to settle down. At this point, I really didn't care to hear his apology. I had already closed the door to that chapter of my life and moved on. I held no anger against him. I figure that his apology to me was to give him closure and allow him to make peace regarding our past.

CHAPTER 4

Age Ain't Nothing But A Number

(Romans 12:9 "Love must be sincere. Hate what is evil; cling to what is good". NIV)

Around the summer of 1998, I was still attending community college. I wanted to get a job to pay for my school expenses because I had a fear of school loans. So, I worked a full time job in the morning and went to school at night. I was an adult now and had to take on adult responsibilities. Ugh, I sure wasn't ready for that. Thank God my cousin let me move in with her to help me in my transitioning process from teenager to adult. I felt free from the older child syndrome at this point, but I really did not want the responsibilities of paying bills. I worked at the local light rail station in the day time. It was there that I met Bernard. Bernard was some type of mechanic at the light rail station. Look I don't know his technical job title, but I knew the brother was making money. The crazy thing is that I was never concerned about how much money he was making. I never was the type of female concerned with the materialistic things. I just wanted that "Real Love" (in my Mary J. Blige voice). So let's get back to Bernard.

There he was, walking into the shop. It was not hard to notice him as there were only two black male mechanics. On the contrary, I don't even think he noticed me. Anyway, Bernard was tall, brown skin, and slim. The first time he walked in the shop I was too busy working, so I could not do anything for him to notice me. Later that afternoon, I was getting on the elevator to check on my staff. Who walked onto the elevator before the door could close? Yes, it was Bernard and his fine self. We spoke to each other and introduced ourselves to one another. The door opened and he said, "Have a good day." I replied, "Same to you."

The next day I did not see Bernard. I was thinking to myself, "Did the brother get fired?" I wondered if Bernard and I would ever cross paths again. Well, I didn't have to wonder long because the following work day Bernard was there. He was looking good. He saw me and spoke, which led to a long conversation. We eventually went out for dinner. He picked me up from my house. I had on a pair of capri jeans, a flowy top, and my flat sandals. My hair was in a pin-up hairstyle, and he had his own little style going on. I almost forgot to mention that Bernard was ten years older than me. I know you're thinking, 'here we go again'. You see, it was a little different. He had his own thing going on. He had his own house, car, and a nice job. He had things that guys I dated before didn't have. It may appear to some on the outside that I was seeking older men to replace the void from the lack of my dad's presence in my life. This was not the case. It was actually new to me. I drove his car and was cooking dinner at his house. We spent a great deal of time together. We never really saw each other at work because Bernard changed his schedule. Some co-workers always wondered what was going on, but we kept it as low key as possible. It was after this relationship that I vowed not to date anyone else that I worked with.

One day Bernard told me that his pastor was coming from another country and needed a place to stay. His church was in the "rebuilding phase". The pastor staying at Bernard's house didn't faze me until the pastor decided to speak his piece. I was in the kitchen one evening making spaghetti. The pastor apparently informed Bernard that we should not be "shacking up". According to the pastor, we were not married and breaking God's law. I told Bernard that I would leave, but it was mighty interesting that the pastor said all of this after he ate my good spaghetti and garlic bread. Oh, he won't get another plate from me. I gathered my things and left the house. I wasn't mad. I was just ticked off because I was trying to figure out how this man was telling us what to do when his own situation was a mess. I have learned it is important to focus on your status before you try to check someone about theirs. Bernard and I still continued to see each other until the unexpected happened. Now, Bernard was a nice guy, but he carried a secret. A few months later, I went to Bernard's house for what I thought was dinner. Yes, the pastor was still living there. Bernard told me at dinner that we could no longer be in a relationship. I was caught off guard, but I did not cry. I was curious for Bernard's rationale for not wanting to continue the relationship. We were together for a year and never had one argument or disagreement. This was strange considering most relationships have challenges, but not this one.

Then he laid it on me. "I promised a woman in South Carolina that I would marry her when we became older."

In my mind, I said to myself, *Are we arranging marriages now in the United States?*" My initial response was "What"? But I replied, "Okay," and took the rest of my things from his home and left. I was not hurt by the break up. I often wondered why I never had a deeper reaction because any other time I would have went off. This left me puzzled for a while.

Almost ten years later, marriages, and divorces, Bernard and I linked back up, courtesy of my sister's Facebook page. We talked and discovered some common things occurred in our lives over the ten year period. We both were divorced and unknowingly lived in the same area at one point. Yes, he had married Miss South Carolina. Bernard relocated to another state, but came back to visit. It's amazing how life will cause you to cross paths again with your past. We went out for dinner. The conversation went well. He apologized for how he ended things. I accepted his apology, but still needed clarity. I didn't understand why a person would walk away from a year-long relationship with the understanding of no issues existing. I thought maybe his family didn't like me and influenced his decision. Well, the secret was about to be revealed. I had to pause and sip my tea for this one.

He left me because deep down inside, our age difference bothered him. My response was, "So your family didn't have an issue with me?"

He replied, "No. It was me."

I was relieved, but I began to understand things clearer. He was concerned with how others perceived us rather than focusing on how we perceived each other. Even after he revealed his truth, I still was not mad or hurt. I finally realized why. At that time in my life, it didn't bother me when he dropped the first whammy because I loved the thought of the relationship and having the comfort of a man. I cared for him; however, I was not in love with him. Far too often, we settle for just the appetizer instead of the full course meal with dessert. The beauty of it all is that we developed a great friendship and still remain good friends even still today.

CHAPTER 5

The Storm

(1 Corinthians 13:4-7 "Love is patient, love is kind. It does not envy, it does not boast, it is not proud. It does not dishonor others, it is not self-seeking, it is not easily angered, and it keeps no record of wrongs. Love does not delight in evil but rejoices with the truth. It always protects, always trusts, always hopes, always perseveres" NIV)

After my relationship with Bernard ended, I was determined to just focus on completing my college courses. While I was in college, I met this cool guy, Marlon. He was in a relationship at the time and we were strictly just friends. I wasn't even looking for a relationship. It was three of us that hung together on the days we had evening classes. I always thought he was interested in the young lady that hung with us. She was pretty and they seem to have had a good connection. I believed she was in a relationship and saw him as just a friend, too.

Marlon and I would talk on the phone here and there. I was still just dating occasionally. As the class was coming to an end, Marlon stopped showing up. This was possibly my first sign when I reflect on it all. Marlon eventually left his relationship and shortly after we began our relationship. We shared our dreams and life plans with each other. It seemed like things would go in the right direction. We continued to date and eventually decided to move in together after years of dating. This was a mistake on my part. Never move in with someone if you can't afford to carry the financial load on your own. Anyway, Marlon seemed excited about us moving in together. Well, that changed quickly. I literally moved in and the next day he told me that he did not want us to live together. I was hurt and confused at the same time. I told Marlon to give me a week to find a place to stay and remove my things from his home. No, I never put my name on the lease. I called my aunt and asked her if I could I stay at her house. My aunt came back in town and helped me move my things. I just wanted to leave in a peaceful way without making contact with him; however, Marlon called my phone. I only answered the call because I thought he was just checking to make sure I was gone before he came home. That was not even the case. This fool had the nerve to call me and try to convince me to not move. I was so confused because before he was very adamant about us living separately. I wondered if there was another woman in the picture or if he was just scared of the change. I opted not to return because I was not about to move my things again. As I'm heading to my aunt's house, she was fussing about the craziness that was going on. My aunt was so angry and the look on her face alone could have killed him. Marlon and I still continued with our relationship, but we just did not live together. Marlon was so back and forth with different things in our relationship and in life. I was strongly debating on leaving the relationship all together. My sister called me and told me not to leave and to just be patient. I wasn't trying to hear it, but then she said the words that every young girl wants to hear. She said, "Marlon wants to marry you. He has the ring and is planning everything." I was shocked and thought maybe I was wrong for making a hasty decision to leave the relationship.

It was Christmas 2000. We were at my uncle's house and Marlon popped the question. The ring was beautiful, and I said yes. For years, I wondered why I never had that "typical" reaction as most women who receive a proposal. I didn't jump up and down, cry, or scream. I just said yes, smiled, and embraced Marlon with a hug. My family was happy for me. As I look back on it, the real question was, "Am I happy for me?" One thing is that we married at a young age and as you mature, things fall into perspective. You see, I did love Marlon, but I was in love with the thought of being married. Quite frankly, so was he. I believe some marriages reflect that same position today and explain why the divorce rate continues to rise. Anyway, we began looking for a home and planning a wedding. We figured it would be more cost effective to stay with my aunt and save our money.

There was one key problem to our relationship that existed since day one: Marlon's mother. Understand that this was not the only problem. I tried to ignore this problem and thought it would eventually go away. I had always pictured going places with my mother-in-law, cooking dinner, getting recipes, laughing, and learning things about life- but instead, I had inherited the complete opposite. She would call and leave hurtful messages on our voicemail about me. We would go to her house to visit for the holidays and my stomach would always hurt. I dreaded going there. I really tried to make the relationship with my mother-in-law better. In the mist of all the verbal abuse from Marlon's mother, he never defended me. At least, he never defended me in my presence. I felt helpless and in it by myself. Whenever I would share the situation with my friends, they would immediately tell me to lay her out and just give her a piece of my mind. I never could do that because I was never raised to disrespect an older person. In my mind, I kept thinking things would change once we got married. Well, the wedding was getting close and we found a new home. I thought Marlon was getting cold feet because he seemed to always not be interested in the wedding details. I was wrong again and yet this was another sign. As I look back, I should have left when I had the chance. God sends signs at times, yet we don't always heed the warning. Was I waiting for God to come from heaven with a bullhorn saying "Run for your life"? Let's just say God would have done that. The question was would I have listened?

We closed on our home and things seemed to be headed in the right direction. We had a beautiful home, good jobs, and all was well… or was it? Everything that looks good on the outside is not always good on the inside. I always say if the walls could talk- baby, this book would have been written.

Well, the big day was here. The wedding was beautiful, except when Marlon's mother decided to wear an all-black dress to the wedding. I sat in the limousine in disbelief, but not shocked by her actions. At this point, I did not want to give it any attention because I was determined that nothing or no one was going to ruin our big day. One of my sisters passed out during the wedding ceremony. We always laugh and say it was a sign. Even while on the honeymoon, Marlon's mother still left messages on the voicemail and made smart remarks when she would come around. I had to take it. I didn't recognize it for years, but I was actually being verbally and emotionally abused. I guess Marlon couldn't handle me complaining about my issues with his mother to him along with the responsibilities of being married, so he left. It took me a while to understand that no one wants to be in a position of feeling like they have to choose between their spouse and their family. Anyway, I came home from work to a half empty closet and a note on the dresser. The note indicated he was not happy. I was devastated. Marlon would not answer my phone calls. It was around the holidays, and it really hurt to not spend it with the person you loved. I received a surprise call from the person I least expected- his mother. She called and told me to cheer up. She said, "Regardless of what was happening, still celebrate Christmas." She suggested we go together to get Christmas decorations. I picked her up and we went to get the decorations. It was a short and good outing. I could not help but to keep wondering why she was being so nice to me now. Was it because deep down inside she was happy that her son and I were separated? Was it because she was relating to my experience because of some things she went thru in her past relationships? Was it guilt for all the years of how she was nasty to me? Her reason didn't matter to me as I was willing to make things work with her for the sake of trying to save our marriage.

I went home to my empty house. I made myself some hot chocolate and turned on some Christmas music. I thought this would help put me in the mood to decorate. The tree was up, and the other decorations were up; Christmas decorations were complete, but I was not. I sat on my couch and cried. Who wants to spend the holidays alone? I kept replaying things in my head trying to figure out where I went wrong. My thoughts were interrupted with the phone ringing. It was Marlon's mother. She invited me to her house for the holiday dinner. I was skeptical about attending, but I went on and accepted the offer. Why did I do that?

I arrived at her house for dinner; it was an awkward feeling because I knew everyone else knew what was going on. I entered and spoke to everyone. I even spoke to Marlon and he did not speak back. It was as if I did not exist. I decided it would be best for me to leave. I couldn't understand how an individual could be so nasty to a person they claimed to love- let alone their spouse. I went home as I was too hurt to be around my own family. Was it more of me being hurt or more of me being ashamed as to how I would be viewed by my family? Either way, I went home. One of my aunts came to my house to sit with me for a while. The next thing that occurred would be the lowest point in my life and a moment that I am not proud of. Some may wonder why I am willing to share this moment. I am sharing this moment because I believe in being transparent as it can help someone else. Please understand that each of us have or will have a story. I was in a space of depression. There was nothing that a counselor, therapist, or preacher could say to help make me feel whole again.

On this night, I went in the bathroom, and took some pills from my medicine cabinet. Yes, my plan on that night was to take my life. I guess I just wanted the attention of Marlon and for the heartbreak to go away.

I went to the hospital via ambulance. I was so embarrassed because my paramedic was one of the regular customers at the bank I worked for. While in route to the hospital, this white man was telling me his story as he was dealing with a break up, too. As I listen to him, tears are flowing from my eyes and thoughts are racing thru my head. I kept thinking of the reaction of my family and how I made my aunt feel. I was in a selfish moment and made a selfish decision because I never thought of others. Heck, I wasn't even thinking of myself. I don't recall if I ever apologized to my Aunt Jernell for the unnecessary stress I put on her that night (My deepest apologies, Auntie).

A couple of lessons were learned from this horrible moment:

- No man or woman is worth you taking your own life. God created you with a purpose, and times will come when you have to push thru the pain to fulfill *his* purpose.

- Loving and accepting yourself is so valuable to avoid moments like this. The other thing worth noting is that God will use anyone, any time, and any place to speak to you. The color or gender does not matter. God used this paramedic and customer of the bank to speak life to me.

I got some rest that night, and I woke up the next day pissed. I was so angry with myself that I allowed this individual to have that much control over me. This was over the weekend, but I had to face Monday morning. I returned to work not knowing if the paramedic had mentioned anything to anyone about my situation. It is my understanding that he did not. He gets in line and personally waited for me to assist him. I was so nervous that I was intentionally taking a long time with my other customer who was just cashing a check. Finally, I waited on the paramedic. He walked up and said, "I'm glad to see you today and you're looking better than yesterday." I thanked him for his help, encouragement, prayers, and kind words. He asked me to promise him that I would not have a moment like that again. I promised and can happily say it has never happened again. I guess you're wondering what happened to my relationship with Marlon. Well, Marlon returned back to our home. I think he returned because of guilt and not because he wanted to make it work.

Marlon and I still attended church with the look of the perfect couple. Years had passed by and our family began to grow. Marlon's indecisiveness began to play a role in our marriage. One minute he wanted to be married and the next minute he was ready to be single. I never knew when I left for work if I was going to return to a "Dear John" letter. I recall one day being at work and trying to call Marlon to see what he wanted for dinner. I'm calling the house and calling his cell with no answer on either phone. I figured he was just in the house sleeping, but I couldn't help to wonder if he left again. So, I went to the market to get dinner only to come home to another letter. Let's just say I received one letter too many, yet I was still determined to make things work for the sake of my children. You see, I didn't want my children to grow up in a single parent environment; however, as time went on, I realized I had no control over that. You cannot keep someone who does not want to be kept. Furthermore, don't no baby keep a man. I continued to deal with the infidelity, verbal and emotional abuse, and a revolving door. It was not easy to go to work every day or even church with a smile on my face. You know wave your hands and shout hallelujah, yet so broken inside not even a cardiologist can fix you. How do you smile on the outside when your world on the inside is falling apart?

I began to just live in a routine mode. I would get up after only having maybe a maximum of three to four hours of sleep, drive the kids to daycare, go to work, pick the kids up, do my motherly duties, and cry until I fell asleep. No one should live their life this unhappy. I was at a place where I was allowing my unhappiness or brokenness to consume me. It not only was showing on the inside, but also on the outside. My weight began to drop because of the level of stress and slow depression I was falling in. Depression is real. Mental health is real. Silence does not always mean that everything is ok. I recall telling one of my good friends that I wish my marriage was like another couple we both knew. She said, "No, you don't want that because everything is not always the way it seems." I thanked her for the advice years later because it always stuck with me, but initially when she gave me the advice, it bounced around like a ping-pong ball. During a period of our separation, Marlon came to get the kids to spend time with them. The kids were in their rooms taking a nap. Marlon came in and we began to argue. Crazy thing is, I don't even recall what specifically the argument was about. We argued and got into each other's face and continued to exchange words. He pushed me and I fell back onto my glass table. The table broke completely and glass was all over my living room floor. He left and didn't even take the kids with him. In that moment, I was more focused on getting things cleaned up before the kids woke up from their nap. As I cleaned the glass off the floor, tears streamed down my face. I found myself again wiping tears and attempting to put a smile on my face for the sake of my kids. I was sore and noticed I had a few scrapes on my legs and arms. Yet, a few months later I took him back because I didn't want my kids to be without their dad in the home. I never realized that the broken table represented my marriage and most importantly me...BROKEN. The mistake I was making was just settling for just anything to fulfill everyone else, yet still being empty on the inside. What do I mean? I was trying to make it work for my kids, to keep myself from being embarrassed, and because I lost myself in the process. Becoming a wife and mother does not mean you must lose yourself. It should help to contribute in becoming a better you. I also realized that I am my girls' first role model and the first queen they will meet in their life journey. I could not keep settling. Just so you know, everyone gets to a point when they become sick and tired of being sick and tired. Well, I finally reached that point.

The point came when I went to the store to get some things to make dinner. Marlon stayed in the house with the kids. I took his car and left for the store. As I was getting back in the car, I noticed two tickets from the state fair. I immediately became upset and for several reasons. One, I just was tired of the lies and infidelity. I am far from stupid and knew the tickets were for him and another woman. The other thing is he didn't even take his kids to the fair. I sat in his car outside of the house. First, I called Marlon and told him he needed to leave and leave for good. Then, I called my realtor and told him to proceed forward with selling the house. The next day I called my lawyer to see how fast I could proceed with the divorce. I was completely done and ready to proceed on the road to happiness.

CHAPTER 6

I Didn't Know My Own Strength

(Psalm 46:1 "God is our refuge and strength, an ever-present help in trouble." NIV)

Yes, I was tired and unhappy. I recall Marlon asking me for a divorce while I was pregnant with our last child. I guess having a healthy pregnancy was not a major concern for him. I was determined to give him what he was asking for and I did. I filed for divorce. My attorney was very adamant that I should file for child support. I did not feel comfortable with that because I just knew Marlon would always help out with our children. I wasn't setting out to make Marlon suffer or to be vindictive. I kept reminding myself that vengeance belongs to God, but I must be honest. This understanding of God fighting my battles did not come instantly, but as I built my relationship with God. During the most difficult times of my marriage, I drew closer to God. I was always in church, but my relationship with God was not strong enough to weather the storm. In other words, I went to church every Sunday and was marked for "perfect attendance"; however, I was not studying my word daily to understand that God is close to the brokenhearted.

I knew financially I would be in a bind because the household was run based upon two incomes. Yes, I set myself up because I should have factored in being able to maintain on my own. Not to think of divorce going in, but it's because anything can happen. I asked Marlon to at least help me pay the mortgage on the house. I didn't think I was wrong to ask for half considering his name was still on the house and his children were still residing there. He told me to figure it out because he was not doing it. I kept wondering how a person you develop a friendship for years with can be so cold towards you. I called my mother that particular time to help me out. Just like many times in my life she has been there to help me. Hearing "figure it out" kept playing in my head. I knew that I would have to proceed with child support. This made the tension even worse. Marlon would come get the kids and the verbal abuse increased. I recall once he said, "No man would want you because you already had three kids." I took that to heart and began to believe it. It also made me angry. I was angry because my heart was broken, I was left to raise the kids by myself, I was in the process of losing my home, and more. My level of anger towards him was ridiculous. I would literally watch the show "Snapped" to try to figure out ways to physically hurt him. My godmother would call me and the first words out of her mouth, "Turn the television off". She knew me too well. I wanted him to feel the pain that he had caused me. At the time, I believed it was important for me to see him suffer. But, I was missing the fact that I was actually causing more suffering towards myself. In spite of all that was going on, I knew I had to fight to keep myself together. I no longer wanted my marriage to work because I was not happy. I was okay with walking away at this point, because I knew I tried all that I could to make things work. I knew that in order for me to be a better mom and a better me I had to be happy. I came to the conclusion that my marriage was not the first to fail and likely won't be the last. But baby girl, this too shall pass.

The divorce was finalized and I felt partially free. I say partially because I was still battling the financial woes with the house. My house was in the process of being foreclosed as I was behind on my payments. I applied for food stamps and was denied because they said my income was too much. I was robbing Peter to pay Paul and Paulina. I tried everything I could to keep the house until I realized I had to take a loss in order to gain. I was able to sell the house and avoid foreclosure. Despite how bad my finances were at the time, all of my necessities were met. I guess while I was trying to figure it out, God already worked it out. I was reminded in this moment that in spite of all around me going crazy, God still provided. He never left me nor forsook me. I guess he was just adding that to his resume with me, as my Uncle Kevin would say. I finally sold the house and felt completely free. I was so happy that I treated myself to some shrimp fried rice and a half & half. A half & half is a mixture of lemonade and sweet tea. Yes, I drove all the way to the village to get it. Oh and it was good! Yes, I was off to a new beginning and also working toward also becoming financially free. I was focused more on building my relationship with God, my children, and myself. Yes, I had to find me again. Finding yourself again is never an easy process, but a rewarding one in the end.

I returned to college to finish my degree and obtain another degree. I did this while working a full time job and being a mom. I learned thru my pain that in spite of what I was going through, my children needed me. My children give me so much joy and strength. I always say they are my heartbeats. They didn't deserve just any type of me, but they deserve the best version of me. I deserve the best me. I was raising queens and I wanted them to always keep their heads up so their crowns would never fall. I know that every now and then I will have to slightly adjust their crowns with my motherly advice. I believe the seniors call it wisdom.

I vowed never to put their dad down in front of them, nor would I allow anyone else to disrespect him in their presence. I will openly admit that was not always easy to do especially when you know the truth. Far too often, when things don't work out with the child's dad the mother tends to take it out on the children. We as mothers tend to play a game of keep away with the kids. This is the worst thing to do and just adds more drama to your life. I wanted to be free so I always left the door open for my children to have a relationship with their dad. I remember telling him that the relationship established between him and the kids would be based on what he chooses to build. This allows the children to make their own decision in this matter. Marlon had and still has some inconsistencies with getting the kids. There are signs of improvement at times, but then it fades away. My prayer is that it gets better consistently one day.

Yes, everything I listed was a big sign of moving forward and letting go. At least, that's what I thought. I recall my godmother telling me constantly that you must forgive him and let the anger go. I looked at the phone like she was crazy. I'm supposed to forgive the man who left me, mistreated me, and the list can go on. Forgive! What in the ham sandwich? The crazy thing is she was right. You can never truly move forward until you forgive and let go. This was a challenging thing for me. I said I forgave him at the time, but I really didn't. I knew I didn't because just his presence alone would make my skin boil. Yes, I am in church working on strengthening my relationship with God and can't forgive my ex. One second- let's do a spiritual self-check. Have you forgiven the person that hurt you, lied on you, or dragged your name thru the mud? I know it is hard, but seek freedom. Take off your mask. The mask I was wearing was years of hurt, pain, and the unwillingness to forgive. I went to church one Sunday with my mask on, and the message was about forgiveness. Why is it every time you're dealing with something, the sermon seems to always be about you? I had to laugh because I was sitting in church that Sunday saying to myself, "Did Pastor Robinson talk to my godmother?"

I wanted the blessings God had in store for me. I wanted to be free. I wanted to love my enemies in spite of what they did. I wanted to be happy. I wanted all of this and in order to receive it I had to do one thing....FORGIVE. I did just that. I forgave Marlon and told him eventually as well. As soon as I completely let go and forgave him, blessings started to flow in my life. The blessings were coming so quick that I could not believe it. You see forgiveness is a powerful thing. Forgiveness is not for the other person; it is really for you.

Forgiveness brings you peace, gives you joy, and allows you to walk in your truth. No longer did I have to worry about what others thought of me or my marriage. No longer did I have to be ashamed of starting over. My tears were no longer of pain, but of pure joy. I'm not speaking of any type of joy, but the joy that the world can't give you and they can't take it away.

After all this you still want to know how I knew when forgiveness had taken place? Well, he would call and I didn't turn my nose up at the phone. Marlon could come around and no longer did I feel nausea. I was cool; however, there was another person in this journey that I had to forgive. Yes, Marlon's mother. My plan was to never talk to her again. One day I was at work and the receptionist paged me. She said, "You have a call on the line, but it does not sound like a typical customer." I had a puzzled look on my face because I could not think of anyone. I told her to put the call through.

It was Marlon's mother.

As she began to go on a rant, I stopped her. I asked her if she could hear me out, but she kept going. I finally was able to say what I had to say when she asked me a question. I don't even recall half of what she said. I told her that she was nasty to me, she was evil, and I did not deserve the things that she had done to me. I told her that I forgave her and would prefer not to have her negativity in my life because I wanted peace.

The day I divorced Marlon I divorced his mother too. I had to forgive and let it all go because I wanted and still want EVERYTHING that God has for me.

CHAPTER 7

A Piece of the Puzzle

(Matthew 6:14-15 "For if you forgive other people when they sin against you, your Heavenly Father will also forgive you. But if you do not forgive others their sins, your Father will not forgive your sins." NIV)

I never knew where things would go regarding my relationship with my dad, especially once I became an adult. I mean, after high school I forgave him for how he left my mother hanging during my childhood years. I don't think my dad truly knew how angry I was for him leaving my mother with the responsibility of raising me. I was mad because I didn't feel that he put forth a great effort to be in my life. I just wanted my dad's time and to be a daddy's girl. I would hear others talk about their dad and see images on television. I couldn't help but to desire just a taste of what that type of bond would have been like. The crazy thing is my mom forgave him a long time ago and I believe she was the best example of forgiveness that I had; therefore, I knew forgiveness was the only option. It came when I felt the need to truly forgive. I just decided to let the chips fall where they may regarding my relationship with my dad. I was never mad at my dad for not staying with my mom, but I was mad that he left me. I'm actually glad they are not together because I just knew she would have driven him crazy (LOL). In seeing their friendship over the years, it allowed me to accept the way things were over the years. I never heard either of my parents speak negatively of one another.

After I entered community college, I still didn't see or talk to my dad often. I pretty much only saw him at church, holidays, or if my mom would call him on matters she felt he should be aware. Those scenarios didn't occur often because I didn't get into trouble often. I must admit, as an adult, it was a little strange to live around the corner from my dad for a year and not go to his home frequently. I thought we would see each other all the time; however, it didn't go that way. I guess I never extended the invite because I was use to not having him around outside of my "normal times". Once I became engaged, my dad made sure I knew how happy he was for me. We became a little more closer when my wedding was getting near. He helped to contribute to the cost of the wedding and I was grateful for it. Even still in that moment, I didn't want his money. I just wanted his time. It seemed in order to bond with my dad I would need to go to an area that he loves- cooking. I would have dinners or parties at my house and dad would be the chef. My dad is an excellent cook and I often think that is his way of showing his love and his understanding of time.

I still had a sense of curiosity as to why my dad was not more involved in my life than he was. In my opinion, he had an example of a good father in my paternal grandfather. They spent a lot of quality time together and displayed a good father-son relationship. The importance of family was clear on both sides of my family. It wasn't a situation where his father was not in his life and a generational curse was taking place. What was missing from this puzzle? A part of me wanted to know and the other part of me was nervous about opening up old wounds; therefore, I remained silent for a while. I always felt that my dad missed out on so many important things as I was growing up; however, I hoped he would make it up to my kids.

Well, the day finally came for me to give birth to my first born child. My dad made it and brought me a plate of food. I was mad because the midwife told me I could not eat and on top of that the contractions were kicking my butt. So much for eating fried chicken and seafood salad. Need I say that seafood salad is one of my favorites? So imagine being pregnant and being denied your favorite food. I'm just going to let that marinate for a minute (LOL). My ex-husband and stepmother left out the hospital room for a few. This left just my dad and me in the room. I had one of the strongest contractions and could not bear the pain. My dad came to my bedside and held my hand. He asked, "What's wrong"? I replied, "I'm in PAIN!" He pressed the button for the nurse. I could see the panic on his face and in my mind I'm praying he didn't pass out. That would have not been a good look of me on the labor and delivery floor and doctors surrounding him to pick him up off the floor. Trust me that would have been a story to tell at the family gatherings. The nurse came in the room and my dad informed her that I was in pain. The nurse looked at both of us like we were crazy because pain is normal in childbirth. My dad left just before my first child was born because there were limitations on who could be in the delivery room. He was actually in the hospital parking lot about to pull off when I gave birth. For once, I felt a close bond with my dad. He was there for me at a time when I needed him the most. I knew he was nervous, but he stuck in there with me. His presence in that moment was everything. I thought that things were on the right track.

Once I faced marital issues, my dad would call to check on me. He would provide his opinion on things and attempt to offer encouragement as well. He always expressed his disappointment in my marriage failing. He also expressed his disappointment for not being there in my life as he should have. I respected his position and in this moment, I just wanted him to be a grandfather to my children. My dad remarried when I was young and inherited two children. As my sister, step-sisters, and I grew older, we all had children. My sister and I would have conversations on how his biological grandchildren where treated compared to his grandchildren inherited through marriage. It appeared he did more for them and they received more of his time compared to our children. I never said much on the subject to my dad and that was because I had already decided to let the chips fall where they may. I am all for blended families; however, the blending must be equally distributed.

During a conversation with my dad, I discovered that my dad never dealt with his own emotions in areas of his life. I'm not even sure that he realizes that. It is important for all of us to own our truth and walk in it. This allows true healing to take place. My truth is that I forgive my dad for the areas in which he lacked in my life. I love him and would do anything in the world for him. He's my dad and nothing can change that, and that's a part of the puzzle; that I know for sure.

CHAPTER 8

A Few Good Men

(Acts 10:2 "He and all his family were devout and God-fearing; he gave generously to those in need and prayed to God regularly". NIV)

Every experience in my life with a man was not bad. A few of the good men in my life are two of my uncles, Kevin and Maurice. They were always involved in my life since the beginning. My uncles helped with taking me to school and whatever else was needed. There was a point in my life when I thought the help went a little too far. My maternal grandparents lived next door to a convenience store. Everyone in the neighborhood went to this convenience store- and I do mean EVERYONE. Well, no one was home but me and my uncle Kevin. My mother had left for work and I was waiting for my grandmother to come home from work. The moment every girl has to face unexpectedly happened.

Yes, my menstrual cycle.

Why did it have to happen with my uncle in the house? Noooooo!

I remember calling my grandmother at work and explaining to her what happened. She told me to ask my Uncle Kevin to go to the store to get me a pack of sanitary napkins. I was so nervous, but I had no choice. I told my uncle what my grandmother said and he just gave me the money to go get it. I was so embarrassed, but I ran to the store. I get in the store and of all days there were a lot of people in the store. I was standing in an awkward position against the wall because I did not want anyone to know what was going on with me. Heck, I barely could process what was going on with me. It's just different when it happens to you. Anyway, I get to the counter and the Asian owner said, "May I help you?" I whispered, "Sanitary napkins". The owner said, "Which ones?" Please explain to me why she just couldn't give me any type of sanitary napkins. Could she not see the look of fear in my face? I grabbed the sanitary napkins and ran back into the house. My uncle continued to watch television. He probably did not pay me any attention. I guess he felt that was a woman's issue. Interestingly, I always thought it was an issue shared between a mother and her daughter. In reflection, I learned that it was a sign that my uncles would be there for me through it all.

Anyway, my uncles would take us to King's Dominion and other travel spots. They definitely put in time with their nieces and nephews. We took our annual family trip to Virginia for our family reunion. We had fun times, and still continue to.

Two of my uncles were the closest men in my life as I grew older. They were not perfect and had their own flaws, but they were perfect to me. So many times they have shown up in my life to help my children and me. I recall being pregnant with my second child and always calling my Uncle Maurice to make baked turkey wings. I craved baked turkey wings so much when I was pregnant. He made the best turkey wings, but the only problem is he seemed to have stopped cooking once I stopped having babies. I think this matter needs to be discussed at the next family outing. I make it my business every Father's Day to recognize the fatherly role they have played in my life as well as my children's lives. The crazy thing is that the majority of my life, whenever an issue arose such as car break down, house repair issues, or you name it- I automatically would call them. My uncles were there every time I had to move; however, there was this one time when something weird happened, and it's a mystery that remains unsolved. My uncles were moving my round glass table into my new apartment. Everything was going smoothly. We were all laughing and joking. Then, I noticed the table stand, but no glass to put on the stand. They each blamed the other and still do to this day. I wasn't even mad because there is never a dull moment with them. You are guaranteed to laugh. If you're wondering why I never called my dad, I never called my dad because I was so used to calling my uncles. This doesn't mean my dad would not have been there; the truth is that I didn't because I just flowed with the norm. The norm for me was calling my uncles, and still is to this day.

My uncles knew just about everything, but they never knew the truth. This is because my mask covered my truth. They knew my divorce left me hurt and bitter towards men and they knew at times I was struggling financially, but I never gave a lot of details. It could possibly be that they may have known more than what I thought they did. It could have been a case of being quiet so that I can figure things out for myself. Sometimes in life you have to hit rock bottom and work at it on your own to get out. It is in those "pit moments" when all you have left is to trust God. Both of my uncles always pointed out the good in me as well as let me know times when I was wrong. I received a good deal of advice and wisdom from them.

I recall my Uncle Maurice telling me I was going to be okay and would get thru my divorce. His advice was always in the positive and had me leave the conversation with a smile. Our car rides together would always call for a reflection of how far I have come. Sometimes it is good to be still for a moment and reflect on the blessings and all that God has brought you through.

I recall one day my Uncle Maurice and I were discussing a guy I was seeing. My uncle said, "Niecey, remember a person never miss their water until their well runs dry. Just sit back and hold tight." Crazy thing is I heard him, but I didn't hear him. You see sometimes when you are going thru things you pick and choose what you want to hear. The downfall to this is that in doing so you miss the whole point being made. My Uncle Maurice always seemed to use life illustrations to explain things to me. Yes, it was his relationship advice again. He told me to stay on the bus, but most importantly stay on the back of the bus. When you are on the back of the bus, you get to see things more clearly. Don't compare yourself to or focus on a person's exes because they are not on the same level as you. I wondered at times if he gave that specific advice because he was hopeful for me, and he only wanted to see me happy. Or maybe, just maybe, he saw something that I couldn't see yet. It's hard to see clearly when you are in the situation, but being on the outside, the view tends to be a bit clearer.

I was talking to him on the phone one day, and my Uncle Maurice made a statement that shocked the crap out of me. So my uncle was talking and I was listening, trying to take in every piece of advice. I said, "Uncle, I'm listening to everything you said and taking it all in." He replied, "Niecey, don't listen to me- just trust God." He didn't know it, but it brought me to tears. I tear up even now just thinking about it. The message was clear once again. Don't worry about what people say or how things look on the outside, but just trust God because he has the final say. My uncle pointed out how I'm in church- shouting, praising, and leading ministries, but lacked faith at this particular moment.

Ouch, that hurt!

I was shocked because my uncle would not be considered the most spiritual person, but I guess he proved me wrong. Out of all the advice he has ever given me, that is the one that sticks the most. It sticks because it required me to do some searching within myself. I had to realize that I have to trust God in good and bad times. I have to trust God even when I can't trace him-according to the scripture Romans 8:28, "and we know all things work together for good to them that love God and are called according to *his* purpose." Ironic thing is, that is my Uncle Kevin's favorite scripture. I had to get out of the moment of wondering "if God can" and get to a place of "God can if I only believe". I realized the mask was there and I had to own the fact that I was heartbroken from the guy I was seeing and own it. It's okay to stand before a body of believers and say that you are struggling with something, or whatever the matter may be. The reason is because you never know what someone else may be going through. It is important to pray for others as it may just be your prayer that helps get them through the storm.

Now my Uncle Kevin is a jokester as well- yet regarded as the most spiritual within the family. He always gives me that deep advice, which requires a bag of popcorn to assist with reflecting on what he said. In addition, he makes sure to keep it real and puts a spiritual aspect in it as well. He always uses his relationship with his wife as an example when explaining things. I must admit sometimes it gets a little too deep for me. At times, I have to tell my uncle to spare the details (LOL). I always admired my uncle's marriage. I get it may not be perfect; however, the beauty is that they're determined to uphold their vows to each other.

One Sunday while he was teaching, he passed out personal cards to each member in the class. On my card, my uncle provided me with a scripture and indicated that I probably did not expect to have found purpose in my pain. Who would have thought that after all I had endured that there was purpose in it? The purpose was to help someone else along this journey of life. Christ endured his moment on the cross so that we could have eternal life. Are you willing to endure the pain to help someone else?

Even though my Uncle Kevin has his own children, he never neglected to let me know that he loves me too. I always hoped that his children would one day understand what that means to me. My Uncle Kevin would always open up his home for family functions. He is determined to make sure our family stays together. In some families, after Big Mama passes away the family typically falls apart. It generally takes one person to open their home and some good food to begin to put things back together. Oh and need I forget a good spades game to keep things going. (Side note: I miss my spades partner☺). Both of my uncles take spades seriously and talk so much trash while playing. Trust me, it is never a dull moment. My Uncle Kevin also makes sure that a sister is in church. I may miss one Sunday, but let me miss a second Sunday, and he is calling like the school attendance monitor! It is his way of checking on me and making sure things are good. My Uncle Kevin always tries to remind me that chivalry is not dead. As a woman, I should still allow a man to open my car door, and much more. Not only does he tell me, he shows me. My uncle even lets me know that I am beautiful and an amazing woman and mom. He also told me it was okay to let down my guard and to allow myself to be loved again. Once again, that which I thought was hidden was not really hidden. I've been told most of my life that I wear my feelings or emotions on my shoulder. I try often to debate it, but it is true. The good thing is they are still actively involved in my life today.

CHAPTER 9

My Bestie

(James 2:23 "And the scripture was fulfilled which says, Abraham believed God, and it was accounted to him for righteousness. And he was called the friend of God." NKJV)

In some cases, it is perceived that a man and a woman can not have a platonic friendship. I used to have that same thought process until I was able to develop a friendship with Terrance. I met Terrance while I was in high school on the number 23 bus coming home from school. Terrance actually went to the same school as my high school boyfriend and they were pretty cool. Terrance and I would have hilarious conversations over the phone. We could talk about any subject from religion to politics to relationships. It was truly a genuine friendship. After high school, we both went to college. We did not talk as much because life became busy with work and school, but when I would see Terrance when he came in the bank to cash his check, things seemed to pick up right where they left off as if we were just on the phone.

One day, Terrance came into the bank as usual on his payday, and I had informed him that I was engaged. He said congratulations; however, I know him and his body language expressed the opposite. He assured me that he was cool and happy for me. Life continued to go forward for Terrance as well as for me. We didn't talk as much as we used to once I got married. I never thought anything of it because I knew we would always be there for each other no matter what. It was just the type of friendship we had displayed over the years. In addition, we had the type of friendship in which we would be direct or blunt with one another. I prefer to simply call it a form of honest communication. As I endured my separation and divorce, Terrance was there every time I called, even if it was simply just to listen. As close as we were as friends, I never told Terrance about the physical abuse I endured during my marriage. He only knew of the emotional and verbal abuse. I never told Terrance about the physical because I knew that physical abuse was not an area he played about.

Years would continue to pass by. We both had children and life was going pretty good. One day Terrance and I were having a typical conversation via the phone. Somehow we got on the subject about relationships and he began to describe my good qualities. I didn't know where he was leading to with the conversation. He finally came out and asked if we could take our friendship further and pursue a relationship. I was shocked because I just was not expecting it. I declined to pursue things any further as I did not want to ruin the great friendship that we had. The best part of that conversation was that we respected the choice to remain best friends and vowed to always keep it real with each other. There were no hard feelings and our conversations as well as friendship continued until things took a turn.

Terrance and I always had this rule in place since high school. If we did not receive a response from a phone call within one day, we would call the other's mother. This one time I didn't stick to the rule at hand. I just assumed he was busy and continued to wait a return call. Finally, day two comes and I received a call from Terrance. I could hear in his voice that something was not right and the tone of my voice changed to that of concern. He told me that he was in the hospital and was in a lot of pain. The medical staff were running test and he would keep me posted. I got off the phone and just sat for a moment confused because everything seemed well the week before. Terrance came home from the hospital the next day even though he was still in pain. He called to provide me with an update and with news that would change our friendship going forward.

Terrance had been diagnosed with a rare form of cancer and he was at stage four. I was shocked and hurt in the same breath. I remember telling him that he was going to get thru it and to remain positive. I honestly didn't know how to approach our conversations at this point because I always wanted to just keep the subject matter on his health status. Terrance asked me to keep things the same and let me know it was okay to talk about things in my life as it helped him not focus on his health issues. So, we continued our "Dr. Phil" and "Oprah" moments. Those were our therapeutic names for each other because that's how deep the advice was when it came to how we should view things in relationships. One thing about Terrance is he had no problem telling me when I was wrong- which was probably most of the time.

It was around Thanksgiving 2017 and I received a message from Terrance indicating to come see him, as he was in the hospital. He actually scared me because he told me I should really make it my business to come to the hospital. I thought he was trying to tell me it was close to the end for him; because we have always been up front with each other, I asked if that is what he was trying to tell me. He said, "No". I ended up making it to the hospital and we were acting silly as usual. Terrance was frustrated at times with his health and this particular day he was focusing on other things outside of his health. I recall telling him to not let people stress him out and to focus on the positive things surrounding him. I said, "We are going to play cancer like football, since it is your favorite sport. God is your quarterback and you are the running back. I want you to run all the way until you get to the finish line. When you get too tired to run, I will be there to cheer you on to the finish line because you will beat this cancer!" It was a very emotional moment for me because I sat there and thought about my aunt, Vanessa, and my friend, Tas, who lost their battles with cancer. In my mind, I'm like, 'not again God'. Terrance replied, "Ok big head," which turned the tears of sadness to tears of joy. I continued to check on Terrance and his condition began to deteriorate, yet he was a fighter and still concerned with how things were in my world. Despite the things I was dealing with I wanted to keep the focus on him.

I was at my children's concert when I received a text indicating Terrance had passed away. I knew it was approaching as I was in constant communication with his family; however, to actually hear it was surreal. It hurt, of course, yet I still was a little numb to the thought of my best friend being gone. It hit when I had a dating question and I wanted to get his male perspective on it as usual. I was in the car and went to pull his name up in my phone and that's when reality hit. I pulled into a shopping center parking lot and cried because I no longer had my best friend to talk to. Who was going to hear my crazy stories and give me relationship advice from a male perspective now?

This chapter is important to include because it is possible for people of the opposite sex to remain strictly friends. I had decided at one point to not include this chapter; however, I decided to because not many people can say they had a true friendship for more than 20 years. The best advice Terrance ever gave me was to always love myself and that advice I have held even closer since his passing. I have learned to deal with death in knowing that God remains in control and makes no mistakes. There is still a lesson to be learned even in death, so fly high, bestie.

CHAPTER 10

Not Again

(Romans 8:28 "And we know that in all things God works for the good of those who love him, who have been called according to his purpose" NIV)

There is one status that sounds good, but really is a dangerous territory. It's called friends with benefits. Oh, it's good and sounds manageable until feelings get involved. In some cases, the feelings may just be one sided. I once heard that no two people will love the same way at the same time. Is that true?

It was a nice summer day and I was headed to get my children from school. My co-worker and I were driving by Druid Hill Park. When it's nice outside, Druid Hill Park always has nice scenery. From the people to the farmer's market, there's never a dull moment in the summer. There was this company doing a volunteer service outside near Druid Hill Park. I noticed this nice looking guy, Mark, who was one of the volunteers. He was really nice looking and I never thought our paths would cross. I guess I was wrong. A few months later, I went to a comedy show with some friends and to my surprise, the nice looking guy was at the comedy show. I thought this was too good to be true. I didn't get his number at the time because I was informed he had a girlfriend. Some time passed, and Mark and his girlfriend were no longer in a relationship, according to him.

We eventually exchanged numbers and began building a friendship. We hung out and one night of fun changed the dynamics of our friendship unexpectedly to add the benefits portion. Mark informed me that he did not want to pursue a relationship at the time because he did not want the responsibility of a commitment; however, we began to spend a lot of time together. We spent so much time together that my emotions began to get involved and I assumed his did too. Well, you know what they say about people when they assume. The time we shared and the chemistry we displayed caused people to begin to speculate if we were in a relationship. I should have walked away then; however, I held onto his actions displayed throughout the years and words from a conversation we later had. Mark said if he was ready to settle down in a relationship, he would settle down with me. I took that as there was potential for things to blossom into a committed relationship, as well as his actions over the years; however, there was a secret that would hold us back. It was a secret that I knew nothing about until the final years, which was too late.

We continued to spend time together and were involved in each other's lives. So much so that people automatically labeled us as a couple. I couldn't blame them because we did things that couples do; however, I always made sure people knew we were not a couple. Mark seemed to be busy a lot, which led to me asking him questions based upon my gut feeling. You know those female intuition questions like, *Are you interested in anyone else? Are you sexually involved with anyone else? Does your heart belong to someone else? Are you in love with anyone else? Do you still desire to be with your ex?*

His answer was always no and that I was over-analyzing things. I decided to take his word because I trusted him, I do secretly over-analyze things, and mostly I loved him. It is hard to detach from someone when you're in love. Some women tend to lead with their heart because we are emotional beings and in leading with your heart first, it can position you for a heart break.

We continued to see each other, and things went downhill in the end of year three. Mark was a ladies' man and always had women leaving comments on his social media pages. I couldn't blame the women because he was fine and a smooth

Casanova. I knew he had female friends, but I did not think the benefits applied. Why? Because I asked him and his answer was always no and I was the only woman he was intimate with. I know, silly me, but the old saying is, love makes you do crazy things.

The initial shift came when I discovered a woman making a false statement regarding Mark one morning as I left his house. When the information was disclosed, I was so hurt that I became numb. I drove around that day to take time to myself to try and process everything. My phone rings, and it's Mark. He tried to explain, apologize, and blame me all in the same breath for his poor judgment. I was willing to listen to his explanation and accept the apology, but when he decided to blame me I forgot everything he said. "How dare he blame me!" was my polite way of thinking at the time. My numbness turned to anger and I just let him have it. Let's just say every word that came out of my mouth was not holy and God would not have been pleased. I was so angry I could have slashed his tires and busted some windows, but I decided to take the high road. A few weeks had passed, but my hurt did not. I continued to pray and look to God for guidance. The question is- was I truly listening. Mark and I decided to sit down to discuss the matter with level heads. It was determined the allegations were false; however, I still held Mark accountable for putting us in a dangerous situation. We continued to hang out, but I noticed that we would always seem to have a disagreement. His argument was I was pressuring him to be in a committed relationship. My argument was I wanted honesty because I felt as if it had been broken. For me, honesty is the foundation of any relationship- whether it's family, significant other, or friends. Every house is built on a strong foundation. If the foundation sustains a crack, water will begin to seep in. It's similar to trust in any type of relationship. One situation placed a crack in our friendship. We tried to work on repairing the friendship, but that was challenging for me because my feelings were deeply involved and I was finding it hard to forget about the false allegations. I guess in hind sight, it was challenging for Mark as well because he was still holding on to his secret.

I was at a place of confusion because I wanted to work on saving our friendship because he meant the world to me; however, I felt that he was keeping something from me. By this time, we had removed the benefits part of our relationship, but my feelings had not been removed. Everything was still a bit fresh. It is easy to fall in love, but seems harder to fall out.

A few days after Valentine's Day, I received a call from Mark. I think by far this was one of the worse arguments we had. I confronted him about a post on social media involving his ex that I was informed about from my stepsister. Why confront him if the benefits disappeared? I confronted him because two weeks prior he was at my house indicating he did not want to be in a relationship with anyone and wanted to be free to do what he wants with whomever. I began to express to him things that he said verbally that were hurtful. As usual, Mark had an excuse for everything. There are times when I felt that he only looked at things from his perspective and never willing to take ownership for his role in any situation. I just left the matter alone.

A month and a half later, I had experienced the loss of a loved one. Mark returned my call to express his condolences. During this conversation, he revealed to me that he was still in love with his exes. This was the secret he had been keeping all this time. I had so many mixed emotions at the time and truly felt as if my feelings didn't even matter. I was quiet on the phone and continued to listen to him. At the same time, I remembered when I asked him about this before and his response was always no. The crazy thing was, I'm not sure if Mark truly understood how I felt- considering he excused himself from the matter by indicating he told me from the beginning that he did not want a relationship. I truly agreed that he did tell me from the beginning; however, his actions said different. He never said I don't want to be in a relationship because I am in love with someone else or have unresolved feelings. It was as if he took my heart and my feelings and played with them. I guess you could call him a mixologist, because he sent mixed signals. The Bible teaches us that the power of life and death is in the tongue. In other words, I should have taken him at his word and not his actions. I believe Maya Angelou said it best, "when someone shows you who they are, believe them the first time". I decided to continue on focusing on rebuilding strictly a friendship and respect his relationship decision, but then the ultimate happened a week later.

I was in church and received a text inquiring if Mark was engaged. I was confused by the text, so I checked Facebook. There it was, bold as can be that he was engaged. I was hurt, shocked, and numb all at the same time. It was as if he knew all along what he wanted to do during the three and half years we dealt with each other. I just felt that if he cared, loved, and respected me as indicated, the courtesy of letting me know up front would have been nice. I mean, after all- we were supposed to be friends and "friends" is not a title I give to everyone. In letting me know up front, it would not have changed my feelings of being hurt; however, I could respect his decision as him telling me versus finding out on social media. I was very hurt and pretty much informed by others that Mark felt he did nothing wrong because we were not in a "committed relationship". It was his thought that I brought this on myself. He sent me a few text messages and I opted not to respond because I was hurt. There was no other way to put it. I guess Mark felt disrespected because of my lack of response to his messages. He sent me a message that I have a pointless and unnecessary beef with him and I needed to get over myself. He would still be there as a friend when needed. I guess he forgot the fact that I was hurt, I have feelings, he was not fully honest, and everything was still fresh. This message was a hit below the belt. I cried and became so angry. I began to wonder if I even mattered at all to him. I began to have a thousand plus questions and thoughts run through my head. According to Mark, he just told me a half-truth about things. I was once told a half-truth is equivalent to a whole lie. I tried to find something to do to change my thoughts. I listened to this sermon and the preacher said, "This is not your battle to fight". I cried even more and asked God to help me. At this point, it was clear that he made his decision and I made mine. My decision was to move on with my life and to continue to seek the things God has in store for me. It is important to know that in moving forward, I had sleepless nights, I would drive in my car with tears flowing down my face, and among other things. Change doesn't happen overnight and you don't just let go that quickly when the love is real.

In my reflection moments, I had to accept the reality of the role I played in bringing some of this hurt on me. I knew

I had to also forgive myself for my poor decisions, which is important. I guess all the times when Mark rejected us being in a committed relationship, it was really God protecting me from an even greater pain. I found myself at a place again where I knew I needed to regroup and refocus. I needed to refocus on what mattered the most- ME. Fantasia sings it best, "I am who I am today because God used my mistakes. He worked them for my good, like no one else ever could. God told me to tell you- it was necessary." The pain was necessary in order to fully understand my purpose in life. The pain was necessary so that I could share my life lessons with my children to help them avoid similar mistakes. The pain was necessary so that I could help someone else in their storm. The pain was necessary so that I could understand the power of forgiveness. The pain was necessary for me to understand there is a time for everything. People are placed in your life for a season or a lifetime. Time will tell which purpose they served in your life. In the end, it must work out for my good.

CHAPTER 11

The One

(Psalm 139:14 "I praise you because I am fearfully and wonderfully made; your works are wonderful, I know that full well". NIV)

My first encounter with "The One" was when I was about 14 years old. I had been around "The One" since birth; however, this time it was personal. Who is "The One?" I found out that he is my way maker, miracle worker, friend, confidant, comforter, restorer, redeemer, my savior, and so much more. "The One" is none other than Jesus. In this encounter, I gave the preacher my hand and God my heart. It was an emotional decision, yet a decision that I still did not recognize the significance of at my young age. It is one decision in my life that I can honestly say that I do not regret.

I continued to live my life as a teenager and was in church every Sunday. I joined the youth usher board, but that didn't last too long. I did not like standing too long and did not greet others with a smile. I guess that wasn't my calling (LOL). The beautiful thing about growing up in church is that it plants a seed in your heart, even if you go astray.

The seed planted led me to stay in church and connected to God. I began to develop an in depth knowledge of the Bible through the young female ministry. During this time, I was engaged, but still not deeply connected to fully understand certain signs early on. I did not use discernment in situations in my life as I believe my relationship with God was still in the infancy stage. If I did, I would have known that my ex-husband and I were not equally yoked. This could have saved years of physical, emotional, and verbal abuse. Now, as my relationship with God grew, I learned a key ingredient. The God I serve is a jealous God and will not have anyone or anything before him, not even your spouse. This is something we often hear from the pulpit, but when I began to read it for myself it was a shocking moment.

The word says "Do not worship any other god, for the Lord, whose name is Jealous, is a jealous God"- Exodus 34:14 NIV.

Now I did turn to God during those years as always, but I don't believe I turned on my own. See, God has a way of getting your attention when your main focus is not him. He sometimes has to place you in the pit in order to get praise out of you. I had to learn that God wanted more from me than just a part-time, pit praise. I began to praise God for keeping me and my children during my valley low moments. As I began to praise him, worship him, and serve him, I could see myself coming out of the pit. This was simply amazing. What's so amazing? This is amazing because the fact is that God was there with me in my mess and still remains with me today even while delivering the message. God never left my side. I have had family members leave, friends leave, enemies leave, men have left, but God NEVER left my side. I continued to build on my relationship with the understanding that it is a process. In the process, I know that I will not always be perfect on my end. I fall short, I stumble, I have shortcomings, and I sin, yet God remains faithful. Even in *his* faithfulness, I still held back one thing. I was not walking in my truth.

What's my truth?

My truth is for years I wore a mask to church just like many believers today. I could pray from the depth of my soul, I could lead a ministry, I could speak life into someone else's broken situation- yet I was broken. I could ask someone where their faith was, yet I lacked faith of my own when storms arose. I could tell someone to take their burdens to the altar and leave them, yet I was picking mine back up. I could speak someone off the ledge, yet I was dangling there myself. I would tell someone to read a scripture, yet a scripture was the last thing I wanted to hear. I promise you I'm not the only one who has been there. I was coming to church broken, shouting, and leaving back out the door broken. The mask of a smile allowed me to walk around as if all was well. The truth was I could barely walk in my own stilettos of truth. On the bottom of those red bottom shoes was the blood I carried from years of hurt from broken relationships, which began at birth. I knew I could not continue to carry the load of hurt any further, so I sought the one person who never failed me. I sought Jesus.

I began to pray and fast. I began to shift my focus on the problem solver and not my problem. I prayed and stayed in my word. I started my day with devotions, scripture, and prayer to help restore my faith. I had to resort to what I knew worked and who I knew could work it. I asked God to walk with me as I walk in my truth, to mend my broken heart, and to protect my heart. I also asked God to help me forgive those who have hurt me and for me to forgive myself. I understood that this key factor, forgiveness, would be the beginning of my healing process. I understood that forgiveness was more for me than the other person. I learned in order to be victorious in the battle that was consuming me; I had to forgive those who hurt me. I began to view it as such. If God could forgive me for my many sins, why can't I forgive those who hurt me? Yes, our sins hurt God and he still showers us with grace, mercy, and favor, all which are undeserving. I promised God for that alone I would forever be grateful toward him and give him glory daily. No longer was I ashamed of my brokenness.

I woke up one Sunday morning, determined to be healed and was eager to get to the church building. I was eager because the church building is where we are supposed to get our healing, deliverance, and breakthroughs. I was eager to see the potter because this clay needed to be on the wheel to be put back together again. I knew that in order for me to become one with myself, I had to seek the only one, Jesus. There is something sweet about being in his presence.

In having a relationship with God, it does not eliminate you from trials. Oh boy, trust me, I still have trials. Doubt even tries to step in at times; however, I have to remind myself that God is still able. I still get my feelings hurt; however, I have to remind myself that for every tear I shed, God was placing them in a bottle of joy. There are times when I feel alone in situations; however, I have to remind myself that God is right there holding me in the cradle of his arms. The most interesting thing is when God himself sends a reminder and will use the person you least expect.

I recall one day feeling really down as I was washing the dishes. I tried to hold my emotions in because my children were around. I knew my kids could sense something was wrong because I was very quiet. I was so quiet and feeling down, that I did not know my kids had left out of the kitchen. My body was present, but my mind was in deep thought. I turned around and noticed letters spelled out on my refrigerator that said "God Is Able". I was shocked and immediately called the kids down to see who did it. Of course, no one wanted to say anything because they thought they were in trouble. I told them it was okay and they left the kitchen. I began to worship God right there and thank him because he used a child to remind me that he is still the One. I guess God knew I needed another reminder, because a year later, I was sitting in my room. I had some things on my mind and as usual, sorting it out in my head. My daughter walked up to me and hugged me. As she walked away, she said, "Mom, it will all work out for your good." It caught me off guard as it was the last thing I expected her to say. I smiled because God never ceases to amaze me. To God be the Glory!

Made in the USA
Middletown, DE
31 January 2020